WHAT WE WORE

STEWART ROSS

Stewart Ross

STARTING HISTORY

Food We Ate
How We Travelled
Our Family
Our Holidays
Our School
Shopping
What We Wore
Where We Lived

First published in 1991 by
Wayland (Publishers) Ltd
61 Western Road, Hove
East Sussex BN3 1JD

© Copyright 1991 Wayland (Publishers) Ltd

Series Editor: Kathryn Smith
Series Designer: Derek Lee
Picture Research: Shelley Noronha

British Library Cataloguing in Publication Data

Ross, Stewart
What We Wore
1. Great Britain. Social life, history
I. Title   II. Series
941
ISBN 0-7502-0143-6

Typeset by Dorchester Typesetting Group Ltd
Printed and bound in Belgium by Casterman S.A.

ACKNOWLEDGEMENTS

Billie Love 5, 8, 24; Chapel Studios 7 (top), 15 (top), 16, 21 (top), 27 (top); Eye Ubiquitous 9 (Paul Seheult); Girl Guide Association 19 (Terence Donovan); Hulton-Deutsch 6, 10, 13-15 (bottom) 22, 25; Mary Evans *Cover,* 20; Peter Stone 7 (bottom); Popper 11, 26-28; Topham 12, 17-18, 22 (bottom), 23; Wayland Picture Library 4.

Words that appear in **bold** are explained in the glossary on page 31.

Starting History is designed to be used as source material for Key Stage One of the National History Curriculum. The main text and photographs reflect the requirements of AT1 (Understanding history in its setting) and AT3 (Acquiring and evaluating historical information). The personal accounts are intended to introduce different points of view (AT2 – Understanding points of view and interpretations) and suggestions for activities and further research (AT3 – Development of ability to acquire evidence from historical sources) can be found on page 31.

CONTENTS

What sort of clothes do you have on today? Are they like the ones these children are wearing? Perhaps you put on a pair of jeans to play. Do you wear an anorak to keep warm?

This picture was taken in 1934, almost sixty years ago. Were your grandparents alive then?

These children are playing in the country. They are going fishing. Look at their clothes. Are they like the ones you wear? What differences can you see? This book is all about clothes and how they have changed in the last sixty years.

This photograph was taken in 1909. Your grandparents' mum and dad might have been alive then. In those days people who had a lot of money always dressed their children in very smart clothes.

This boy is wearing his best suit. It is made of wool. The wide **collar** on his shirt was very fashionable then. He must have come from a rich family.

Peter Stone works in a post room today. The photograph at the bottom of the page was taken in the 1930s, when he was seven years old. Peter is the boy on the right, holding his granny's hand.

'We had just come home from school when this picture was taken. We had our hair cut very short, so that **lice** wouldn't be able to live in it. Some of the children in my class were very poor. The teachers gave them shoes because their parents could not afford them.'

BABY CLOTHES

This baby was born in 1950. She is dressed in a pretty cardigan made from wool, to keep her warm. Perhaps her grandma knitted it for her. She is wearing a **cotton** nappy. Cotton nappies had to be soaked in hot water for a long time when they got dirty.

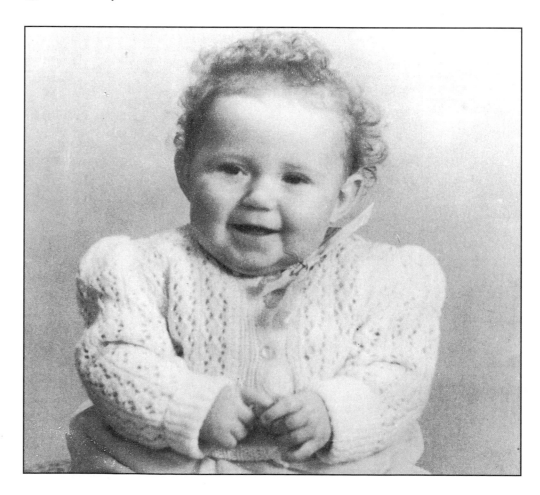

You might have seen a baby wearing a suit like this. It is in one piece, so her tummy does not get cold. There are not many buttons to do up, so her mum or dad can dress her quickly. Her nappy is made from soft paper, like a tissue. When it gets dirty, it is thrown away.

WHAT'S UNDERNEATH?

About sixty years ago, women wore underwear like this. Can you see their **corsets**? Women put on corsets to make themselves look thinner and to hold up their **stockings**.

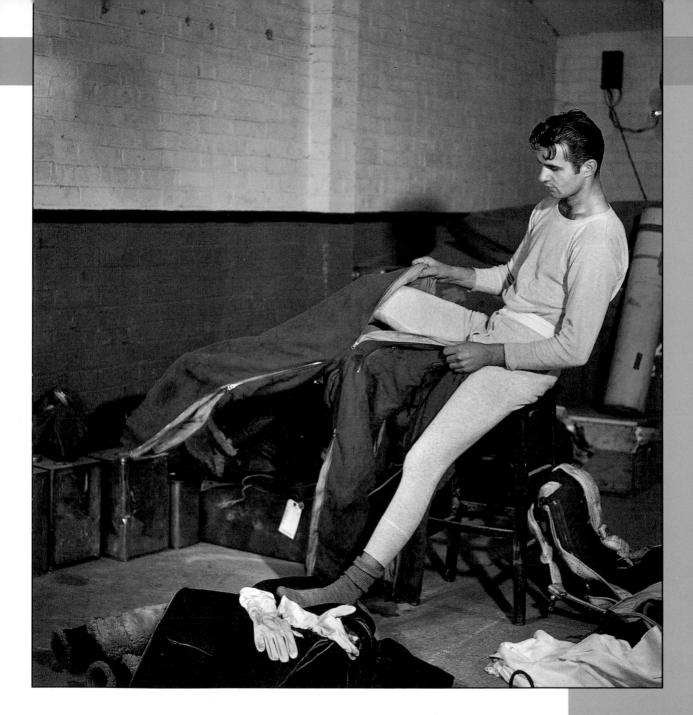

Men used to wear long underpants like
the ones in this picture. They were baggy
and white, and made of cotton or wool.

CLOTHES FOR WORK

What do your parents wear when they go to work? This man worked in an office in London in 1960. He is wearing a bowler hat and a very smart suit. You might have seen people dressed like this in old films.

In the 1950s, women who worked in offices were not allowed to wear trousers. This woman's dress is not very different from the ones people wear today. How can you tell that it is an old picture?

Mr Bird was a farm labourer in 1940. He worked outside all day. He is wearing thick trousers to keep him warm. He also has **leather gaiters** on, to stop his trousers from getting muddy round the ankles.

Millie Kershaw can remember helping her mum wash clothes in the 1930s.

'My dad worked in a factory. His clothes were always really dirty when he came home. Sixty years ago, nobody had a washing machine. I used to help mum wash all the clothes by hand. Then she used to put them through a mangle like the one in the picture below. The mangle squeezed out most of the water. She wouldn't let me use it, in case I squashed my fingers!'

15

Today, people who work outside can wear overalls like these. Overalls are easy to wash. They have no loose pieces that might get caught in machinery. This woman is wearing a hard hat to protect her head too.

In the twentieth **century** many new materials have been invented. This diver's wet suit is made from a material like rubber. It helps him to keep warm, so he can stay longer in the water.

UNIFORMS

Ask your grandparents if they were in the Cubs and Brownies. What were their uniforms like? In the 1960s Brownies wore uniforms like this. For a long time they did not change very much.

In 1990 Brownies started wearing new uniforms. They are still brown and yellow, but the Brownies can choose different tops, trousers and skirts. Do you like the old or the new uniform best?

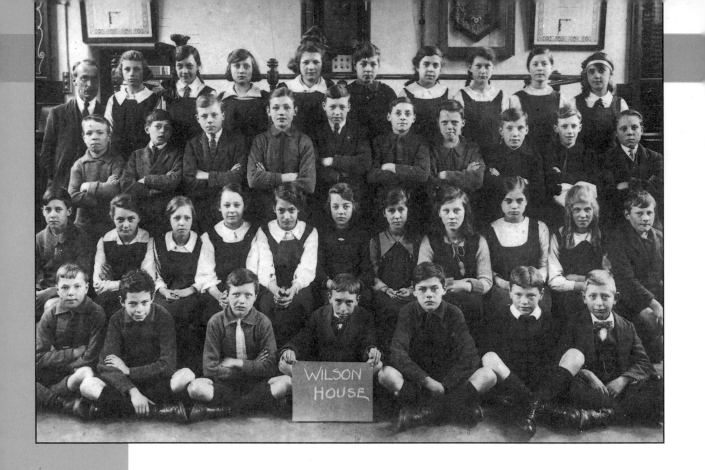

These children are wearing their school uniform. The girls are wearing pinafore dresses. The younger boys are dressed in shorts. Some boys used to wear shorts until they were eighteen years old – even in the winter. Their legs must have been very cold. Can you see any bow ties?

School uniforms are more sensible now. Some schools don't have them at all. Do you wear a uniform for school?

Some people wear uniforms at work. Jack Walker was a firefighter in London during the **Second World War**. He wore a uniform like the one below.

'I wore rubber trousers to keep my legs dry. I got very hot in them. We all had to wear tin hats too. Mine was too big. It kept slipping down and banging me on the nose!'

Suzanne Lenglen was a famous tennis player in the 1920s. Look at her long skirt. She is wearing stockings and leather shoes.

She must have been very hot running around in all those clothes. In those days, people were shocked if a woman showed her bare legs.

Today women wear short skirts or shorts for playing sport. They are much easier to move around in. Modern sports shoes help people to run fast. Do you have a pair of trainers or plimsolls for PE?

Look at these men in their swimming
costumes! Men don't wear clothes like
these for swimming today. This
photograph was taken in 1931.

Footballers' clothes have changed in the last sixty years too. These men are dressed in long baggy shorts. The referee is wearing a **waistcoat** and jacket. They look funny with his shorts!

PARTY TIME

This young woman is dressed up in her party clothes. She is from a rich family and she is going to a **ball**. Dresses with wide skirts were very fashionable in the 1950s.

Fashions changed very quickly in the 1960s. Many older people did not like the clothes that teenagers were wearing. Lucy White can remember going to parties in clothes like those in the picture below.

'My mum was very cross when I went out. She said my skirt was too short and I was wearing too much make-up. When I was a bit older, I had a boyfriend who had long hair and wore beads. My dad said he was a **hippie** and threw him out.'

These children are playing games at a
birthday party. The photograph was taken
in the 1950s. Do you wear clothes like
these for your friends' parties? Can you see
any clothes that are different from the
clothes you wear today?

Have you been to a party like this one? Everyone is dressed up and having a good time. People have always enjoyed dressing up for parties!

FINDING OUT MORE

Talking to people

Ask grown-ups you know well about the clothes they used to wear. They might be able to show you some of the old clothes they have kept.

Using your eyes

Old books, papers and magazines can tell you what people used to wear. Look at the clothes people are wearing in old films. Films and paintings can help you to find out what people wore hundreds of years ago too.

Clothes on display

You might like to make a history scrapbook or display about clothes. Start with the clothes people wore ten years ago. Then look at clothes from twenty years ago. See how far back you can go.

Read all about it

The pictures in these books will help you to find out more about clothes from the past:

A Family In The Thirties Sue Crawford (Wayland, 1988)

Looking Back: Clothes and Fashion Joanne Jessop (Wayland, 1991)

Family Life in World War Two Gary Patrick (Wayland, 1990)

When I Was Young: The Sixties Richard Tames (Franklin Watts, 1990)

When I Was Young: The Seventies Neil Thomson (Franklin Watts, 1990)

When I Was Young: Early Twentieth Century Ruth Thomson (Franklin Watts, 1989)

GLOSSARY

Ball   A smart party where people dance. Women usually wear long dresses and men wear dark suits and bow ties.

Century   One hundred years. The twentieth century, which we are living in now, began in 1901 and will end in the year 2000.

Collar   A piece of material round the neck of a shirt or coat.

Corsets   A tight vest which women wore round their tummies. Some corsets had hard bone inside them to make them even stronger.

Cotton   A material that is made from the cotton plant.

Hippie   Somebody who is against war. They have long hair and bright flowery clothes.

Leather Gaiters   Coverings to protect the legs below the knees. They are made from animal skin, which is a strong smooth material.

Lice   Insects that live in people's hair. They bite the scalp to suck blood and this makes the head itch.

Second World War   The war that took place between 1939 and 1945. Britain, the USA and the USSR, helped by many other countries, fought against Germany, Italy and Japan.

Stocking   A close-fitting knitted covering for the foot and leg.

Waistcoat   A sleeveless jacket, often worn underneath a normal jacket.

INDEX